To Sally,
a fellow dog Lover.

Waggin' Tales: Bogey's Memoir

Hugs,

Maureen O'Brien

Waggin' Tales:

Bogey's Memoir

Maureen O'Brien

Waggin' Tales: Bogey's Memoir

For information contact:
mobrienauthor@aol.com

Cover photo by Maureen O'Brien
Cover design by Janice Ranum
Author Photo: June Jordan

ISBN-13: 978-1500615826
ISBN-10: 150061582X

First Edition: September 2014

10 9 8 7 6 5 4 3 2 1

WAGGIN' TALES IS POIGNANT AND INSPIRING. It is a bridge between the harsh world in which we live and the compassionate and tender side of our humanity that often gets lost in the shuffle. A must read for anyone age 4 to 104 who has ever loved a dog.

Rick Kaplan, President
Canine Angels Service Dogs

BOGEY'S MEMOIR IS THE TALE OF A FUN-loving, brilliant toy poodle, dubbed from birth by his first owners as untrainable and stupid. Adopted by a loving family, Bogey is transformed and becomes "the smartest of them all," receiving many awards to prove it. Through a blend of captivating storytelling, the reader is taken into Bogey's world and is enveloped by the candor, honesty, suffering and happiness that only "sweet baby Bogey" can portray. Bogey's adventures take the reader through a wide range of emotions on earth, and in heaven. Maureen O'Brien combines humor and sadness to create a first person narrative of caring, sensitivity and insight. This is a story that dog lovers and others will cherish.

Freda M. Peters, Dog lover and
Retired Textron Executive

FOREWORD

When Maureen O'Brien asked me to write the foreword to Waggin' Tales: Bogey's Memoir, I was honored. Throughout my life I have been dedicated to the care and well-being of all God's creatures, large and small. But I must confess that there is a special place in my heart for dogs. I am a passionate dog lover.

I am the Executive Director for Grand Strand Humane Society, Bogey's safe haven, until his Ma and Pa adopted him and gave him a permanent, loving home. Their home was filled with so much love and care that he blossomed into a legendary therapy dog, spreading joy and happiness to children and to the elderly.

After reading Bogey's memoir, I fell in love with him. I will admit that when I came to the chapter, "I See a Colorful Bridge," I had to close the book for a while and stop reading. You see, I had a Cocker Spaniel also named Bogey who crossed the Rainbow Bridge at seventeen years of age. I didn't think I could bear a sad ending. To my amazement the following chapters, where Bogey tells of his life in heaven, are so uplifting that rather than experiencing sadness, my heart filled with joy.

This is a beautiful story between caring humans and an enchanting dog sharing unconditional love. Bogey was special, talented and adorable. The real message I took from the book is no matter how much you love your dog, you can always love another. Our hearts are open even when we think the pain of loss has closed them.

At Grand Strand Humane Society and other rescues and shelters, there are far too many stories like Bogey's... a beautiful, loving dog ends up in a shelter. We have every breed, every size, every color, every age and they all deserve a permanent home with a loving family.

Bogey fell into "the honey pot" when Moe and Lamar adopted him. This is my prayer for every puppy, dog, cat and kitten.

I know you will also fall in love with Bogey as you read his memoir. I hope that his story will lead you to a shelter or rescue to adopt your very own "Bogey."

— Sandy Brown

PREFACE

I knew nothing about the first six months of Bogey's life. Why his prior owners considered him stupid and untrainable was beyond me. What I do know is that he was the most brilliant dog I have ever been blessed to parent. My personal opinion is that there is no such thing as a stupid dog. Like most dogs, all Bogey needed was lots of love which we gave him and which he returned, unconditionally.

Bogey touched so many lives and brought joy and laughter to everyone he met. I hope his memoir will motivate people to consider adopting a homeless animal from a shelter when looking for a pet. I also pray that it will ease the grief for anyone who has lost a beloved pet.

Four days after Bogey crossed the Rainbow Bridge, I took a walk around the block in my neighborhood, the same route that Bogey and I had traveled every day. This wasn't a spur of the moment thing. I had made a deliberate decision the night before to do this as a tribute to him.

Bogey, Bogey, Bogey. I couldn't get him out of my mind. If you've lost a pet, a true member of your family, I'm sure you understand how my mind was galloping. I simply couldn't stop thinking about him.

As I walked out the front door, I found myself looking to heaven and whispering, "I will be strong and will only think about all the wonderful times we've shared. Only good memories, sweet baby boy. I love you, Bogey." Without a leash in hand and without Bogey just two steps ahead of me, I didn't get very far before I began to sob. It wasn't a gentle, quiet cry. I bawled out loud, completely out of control. My only thought was that Bogey was gone forever. Or, so I thought at the moment.

The very next day I wrote the first two stories of *Waggin' Tales: Bogey's Memoir*. I wrote it for me, to help me through my grief. I wrote it for him, so he would be remembered forever. When I finished those stories, I realized that the act of writing down the memories rather than just reliving them in my mind started to give me the peace I so needed. Placing Bogey as the narrator seemed right to me. It allowed me to hear his voice and to listen to his life story, rather than talk about it. Over the next few weeks, I continued to jot down these memories. The more I wrote, the better I felt.

About a year later, I enrolled in a Writer's Roundtable. Our mentor was Trilby "Tibby" Plants, author of *Hubert Little's Great Adventure*, and *Meena Mouse's Perfect Raspberry*. While other Roundtable members submitted their upcoming novels to be critiqued, I submitted my Bogey stories. Quite honestly, I felt a little silly. My narratives weren't exactly the beginning of the great American novel.

To my delight, at the end of one of our sessions, Tibby said, "Moe, Bogey's stories are wonderful. You really should publish them."

That was the furthest thing from my mind. I have Tibby to thank for the book you are holding. I can't thank her enough. She is a wonderful teacher and mentor but more than that, she is a dedicated coach.

When I asked Sandy Brown if she would write the foreword to the book, she said she would be honored to do so. Quite honestly, I was honored that she accepted. Thank you, Sandy.

Special thanks to my friend Dee Senchak, a fellow Roundtable member. She read and re-read every story and made suggestions that were invaluable. All this, while writing her very own novel. I owe her big time and will be right there for her when she's ready to publish. We shared so many laughs throughout this journey. Who would have thought that misplaced commas could provide belly laughs? I love this lady.

Thank you to my friends, Maureen Blanchfield Bellantoni, Peggy Clark and Betty Sandbeck, for reading each individual story, each time I wrote and re-wrote. Their editorial comments kept me motivated and on the right track. They believed in what I was doing and it made a world of difference.

Thank you to my Beta readers, Pat Thompson, Kit Burns and David Griffin. Their suggestions for changes were spot on.

A big thank you to Libby Adams, my friend and sister-in-law for digitizing all my hard copy photos and preparing them for publication.

A heartfelt thanks to my loving, talented sister, Janice Ranum, for creating such a beautiful cover for my book. She always makes me feel so loved.

I will be donating profits from the sale of my book to the Grand Strand Humane Society in Myrtle Beach, SC.

— Maureen O'Brien

CONTENTS

To the two greatest loves of my life:
My husband, Lamar Adams
and my son, Erik Oberhammer.

I can see you right now, giving each other
high fives in heaven.

My love for you is endless.

My Lucky Day

1

"He's untrainable and stupid." That's what I hear my owners tell The Society lady. Can you imagine?

Oops, hold on a minute. I'm getting way ahead of myself here. This is the story of my life and I haven't even introduced myself yet. It's just so hard to get those words out of my head.

My name is Bogey. I'm a six-month-old black, toy poodle, and sad to say, my current home is the Grand Strand Humane Society in Myrtle Beach, South Carolina. Apparently the people I had been living with decided they'd be better off if I were living with someone else.

Being here for the past five days has been anything but fun. First of all, there's no freedom. The only time they let me out of this barren, cement-floored cage is when a lady comes down the hall and says, "Bogey, do you want to go for a walk?" To let her know how desperate I am to get out of here, I jump up against the steel fencing, wag my tail like crazy and then run around in circles. Thank God, the nice lady takes it as a "yes."

The other problem is that there are so many other dogs here. I can smell them all over the place. And there are even more cats. I think those cats must be having babies just about every day. I don't dislike cats at all but I'm wondering how so many of them got in here. The real issue with the cats is that I think I'm allergic to them. I've been sneezing a lot.

Today is St. Patrick's Day so maybe it'll be my lucky day. The head honcho here, not the lady who takes me for walks but the one I call The Society Lady, comes down to my neck of the crates. Wish I could say "neck of the woods" but I only get to smell the sweet scent of grass, and trees, and dirt about four times a day. Anyway, she doesn't say anything about walking. After placing a tether around my neck, she says, "Bogey, how would you like to play with everyone in the lobby again?" Then she walks me down a long hall to the entrance of a glassed-in room. I poke my head around the corner and I see a man and a woman talking to the receptionist. I hear the woman say, "I called yesterday and you said you have a toy poodle named Bogey. May we see him?" I hear my name and so immediately, my ears perk up.

"Of course," the receptionist says. "Perfect timing. Miss Rita just happens to be bringing him down here as we speak.

Maureen O'Brien

We've just started to let him hang out with us in the lobby every once in awhile. He's so darn cute, but I do have to tell you that his prior owners weren't very happy with him. Oh, here's Miss Rita and Bogey now."

The man doesn't even turn to look at me and The Society Lady. Instead, he turns to the woman and in a whisper, but loud enough for me to hear, he says, "See, I told you. I don't want a dog and if you insist on getting a dog, I sure don't want a poodle. Besides, if his prior owners didn't like him, there has to be a good reason. I'm sorry I let you drag me down here. C'mon, let's go. Forget about this."

The man sounds pretty adamant. When I hear these words, I can't help but start to whimper a little. Good grief! What does he have against poodles?

Here's what happens next. The Society Lady starts to walk me over to the woman. I feel a sneeze coming on but I hold it back, on account of, I don't want the woman to think I'm sick. Plus I haven't been groomed in three months. Even I know I don't look like a poodle. Turns out, this is a good thing.

The woman rushes over to me and picks me up in her arms. "Would you look at this baby? He looks nothing like a poodle."

Holding me even tighter, she saunters over to the man and holds me up so I'm almost nose-to-nose with him. I'm thinking, maybe this isn't such a good idea. I mean the man definitely doesn't like dogs. "Look at this little guy. He doesn't even look like a dog. Lamar, this little Bogey looks just like a teddy bear."

I'm feeling good about the woman, but she leaves without me.

A whole week goes by and the people at the Humane Society are being extra nice to me. I think it's because I have this silly cone-shaped thing around my head. Why, I don't know, but it's driving me crazy. They keep telling me I'll feel better soon. One of the volunteers says in a very soothing voice, "Sorry about that buddy but you had to have the surgery." Then I overhear one of them say, "Such a shame. I would have loved to have seen more little Bogeys." I really like the sound of that cause those people I was living with… well, they didn't even like having one little Bogey.

Today I come to the lobby and I'm surprised to see the man and the woman who came last week. They're very busy talking to The Society Lady and scribbling all kinds of stuff on one piece of paper after another. Next thing I know the woman walks over to me and puts a brand new red collar on me. "Oh Bogey. I just knew red was your color. You look so adorable. Would you like to go for a ride in Ma's car?" I cock my head a little and then wag my tail cuz I love going for car rides.

Here I am in the car, sitting on Lamar's lap. I can tell by the way he's holding me that he's trying to get used to the idea of being a dog's Pa. I lie down and stay very quiet – which isn't easy for me. He strokes me a little under the chin and I lick his hand to tell him how much I like that. Then he runs his other hand through the furry curls on my back. I roll

Maureen O'Brien

over on my back so he can give me a belly rub. Lamar looks like he doesn't know quite what to do now.

Ma is driving but she reaches over with one hand to pet me. "Bogey, you are such a good baby." She sounds a little bit like she's purring. I'm thinking we've got a love at first sight thing going on here between Ma and me.

We arrive at what I hope will be my "forever home" and all I see are teddy bears all over the house. It's pretty obvious that my new Ma and Pa are crazy about Teddies. I guess Ma knew just how to describe me. There's no doubt in my mind that before long, the teddy bears will be fading into the past. Actually, they look like neat toys so I hope I'll be allowed to

play with them. And I sure hope they have squeakers inside them. I think I'll wait a bit before I test them out.

Ma shows me around the house, pointing out my food and water bowls and my bed and a basket filled with toys. I think I'm gonna be very happy here. I just hope my new Ma and Pa will keep me.

I'll have to show them very soon how smart I am, especially Pa.

Maureen O'Brien

I always say, friends are the family we choose.
Is it any wonder dogs are called man's best friend?

— *DR*

2 ## POTTY TRAINING

I'm into my second week with Ma and Pa. For a while there I was thinking of them as my new Ma and Pa, but now I just call them Ma and Pa cuz I'm pretty sure they're gonna keep me. Hot Diggety Dog. Just call me Wonder Dog. At least they think so, and I haven't even shown them how smart I am yet.

One thing at a time. Right now, I'm just trying to be good. Being good means not lifting my leg on the couch and definitely, no poopies in the house. And Pa told me about his slippers – no chewing.

Ma is taking Joyce's potty training advice seriously. Joyce is a neighbor down the street who says she was a dog trainer in one of her other lives. Who knows, maybe she used to be a cat too. You know what they say about cats ... something about nine lives. I don't know about you, but I don't really believe that stuff. If anyone deserves nine lives, it should be a dog. Well, maybe both cats and dogs.

Here's how the potty training is going. In the house, Ma keeps me tethered to her on a very short leash and then takes me outside and says, "We're going out for potty." Then when I manage a wee or a poo, Ma goes crazy, praising me. "What a good boy, Bogey. Very good potty." You'd think I did something really smart. Honestly, it just so happens I have to go each time. Perfect timing, I would say.

Anyway, Ma and me are glued together like Velcro. Even when Ma does her business in her bathroom, I am right there with her sitting next to the toilet.

Today, Pa tells Ma that he thinks I should be let loose in the house. "I love this little guy," he says. "And he's pretty darn smart." You can't imagine what his words mean to me.

Here I am fancy free, loose, running around the house and going anywhere I want to go. It's very exciting. I'm having a real adventure until all of a sudden I have to go. I'm thinking here's my chance to show them how smart I really am. So I dash into Ma's bathroom and park myself right in front of the toilet. I do my poopies right there. "Good boy, Bogey," I say to myself.

Next thing I know I hear Ma say, "Pa, where's Bogey?" I'm just finishing my business when she finds me. She starts laughing so hard, she starts crying. "Bogey," she says, "You are one heck of a smart baby boy."

Maybe, Wonder Dog is a good moniker for me.

3   Like Father Like Son

I'm so much like Pa it's not to be believed. Everyone describes him as a True Southern Gentleman. He's very laid back, mild mannered, slow moving, and soft spoken. He mulls things over a whole bunch before making a decision. And he hardly ever gets angry. I guess it all makes sense since he was born and raised in North Carolina.

I'm a Southerner just like Pa. That could probably explain it. But I think it's more than that. Maybe it's cuz I'm home with Pa so much that I favor him. Ma is on the go a lot and she can't always take me with her. I really don't mind cuz I'm a homebody just like Pa. It's funny cuz one of the neighbors who walks by our house always stops to give me pet pets, and I swear, she always says, "Bogey, you are such a gentleman." Makes me feel really good that I'm so much

Maureen O'Brien

like Pa.

When Pa and me go for our walks, I stay right with him. At the most I'll go four steps in front of him, not exactly heeling which I'm not really good at, but I never pull on the leash. I know his pace and it suits me just fine. He lets me sniff everything in sight and pee at every mailbox. There's never a rush. Talk about taking time to smell the flowers. We do that all the time. Well, maybe not the flowers, but for sure the mailboxes.

When we meet someone new, Pa always introduces me as his son. I love him so much.

Some of our greatest historical and artistic treasures we place with curators in museums; others we take for walks.

— *Roger Caras*

The Contest

4

It's the day before Halloween and Ma is trying costumes on me. I'm not enjoying this one bit. I'm letting her know by chewing on anything and everything she puts on me. I've already destroyed a Superman cape. Geez, I hope she didn't spend a lot of money on this stuff. Just think of all the treats she could've bought me instead.

She even tries to put a sailor hat on me. You gotta be kidding. It only takes me ten seconds to get that darn thing off. All I do is roll over and over again on the carpet until the crazy thing falls off. How many other costumes is she gonna try? Even on a cold day, I don't like wearing a sweater or a coat. My own fur coat keeps me plenty warm, thank you very much.

After an hour of this, Pa comes to my rescue. "Honey," he says, "I think it's pretty obvious Bogey doesn't want to wear a costume. Why don't you just let him be? I know it's Halloween and they're giving out prizes for Best Costume. But even without a costume, he can still walk in the dog parade. Anyway, aren't you entering him in the Best Trick contest? You know he'll win that, hands down."

Pa sure sounds pretty confident that I'll win. I do know three tricks but the thought of a contest is really scary. Contest, the word itself is frightening. Besides, I've never been in a contest before and I never did my tricks in front of a lot of people. I'm praying that I won't be too nervous. I want Ma and Pa to be proud of me.

The very next day we are off to the Annual Halloween Dog Parade. It's a benefit for the local Humane Society. Guess what? Just seven months ago, that's where I was living before Ma and Pa adopted me. This benefit raises a bunch of money for all the rescue dogs. I'm happy to do my part for such a good cause.

The first thing that hits me is how many dogs there are. I've never seen so many dogs in all my life. And you know what? They are all so well behaved. I don't hear any crazy barking and not one dog tries to sniff my butt. I really don't like having my butt sniffed.

The next thing that hits me is the number of people. For every dog here, I'll betcha there are at least four people. I mean to tell you, this is some big deal.

It's a very hot and humid day with no breeze whatsoever. So Ma and Pa decide that we won't walk in the full parade, just a little part of it. Right after that, Ma goes over and pays

Maureen O'Brien

the money to enter me in the Best Trick contest. Then we wait forever cuz I'm the last dog to be called onto the stage.

Now this part is just way too funny. One dog gets up there and his owner commands him to roll over. The dog just sits there dumbfounded, staring at the judges. His owner gives him three more commands, to no avail. The dog promptly lies down and puts his head between his paws. That ends that. The next dog up is supposed to shake hands. Instead of doing that, he does a huge poop right on the stage. I mean it's one big poopy doop. Poor guy, I guess he really had to go.

The dog right before me is a little Jack Russell. She's so darn cute. Her owner says, "Ruby, show everyone how pretty you sing." With that, Ruby takes a flying leap off the stage, leaving her owner in the lurch. That girl sure can jump. Too bad her owner didn't tell Ruby to show how good she could jump. She probably would have won the contest. I thought the audience would never stop laughing.

Now Ma and me are introduced. "Last, but not least, we have Maureen O'Brien and her toy poodle, Bogey."

The first thing Ma does is to tell everyone that she and Pa adopted me from the Humane Society just seven months ago. She also tells them that my prior owners gave me up because they thought I was stupid and untrainable. The last thing she says before asking me to do my tricks is, "Take a look at him now." Pretty good job warming up the audience, I'd have to say.

My first two tricks aren't all that dramatic. All I do is sit

up with my paws in the air when Ma asks me to say please. Then she asks me to shake hands. Like I said, not the hardest tricks in the world but I do each of them, right on cue.

My third trick is incredible. At least the audience and the judges think so. Ma announces to everyone that I know how to do math. She then proceeds to ask me to add, subtract, multiply, and divide. I wait and listen intently and then

Maureen O'Brien

bark out the answer. Didn't miss a one.

The audience and the judges give me a standing ovation. Then they hand Ma a plaque that says First Place Best Trick Contest. The first thing Pa does when we get home is to hang the plaque in a prominent place in his den. The plaque is nice and all, but the best part is the basket they gave me, filled with treats and toys.

I don't mean to brag or anything but I went on to win first place in that contest for the next two years. After three years Ma decided not to enter me anymore. She said it wasn't a fair fight cuz I was too smart.

5 MY FIRST BIRTHDAY

It's September 20, 2003, and it's my very first birthday. I can't believe this but Ma and Pa are throwing a party for me. Three of my dog friends are coming, and some of Ma's friends too. Oh my gosh, I can't even let myself think about all the presents. This might be even better than Christmas. I'll find out soon.

The day starts out with Pa decorating the garage with those balloons on a stick that say Happy Birthday. He even ties one to our mailbox so the whole world will know it's my special day. Ma buys party hats for everyone and dog biscuits and bones for all the dogs. She even buys a toy for each dog to take home with them.

Bernie the Beagle is the first dog to arrive. She isn't here five minutes when she tries to steal the present she brought for me. What gives with that? As soon as her Ma says, "No,

Maureen O'Brien

Bernie, no," she's very good and drops the stuffed bone that's in her mouth. Then she dashes over to a pile of presents that Ma has put on a table. Thank God, she can't reach them. Her eyes look so sad though. I kind of feel sorry for her. I don't know if it's a beagle thing or not, but Bernie's eyes almost always look a little sad.

Then my buddy Riley hobbles into the party with his Ma. I'm so happy that he's here cuz he's thirteen years old and sometimes his hips hurt him. I wasn't sure he could make

it to my party. He's always so sweet to me. Riley is a really big golden retriever so Ma gives him a special, big rawhide bone. He just lies down on the floor and munches on his bone.

Next to arrive is my hyper friend, Bridget the Shih Tzu. She doesn't waste any time trying to stir things up. The girl never stops going. She stalks Riley and even jumps on his back trying to get him to play. Riley totally ignores her and keeps munching away. Nothing bothers my buddy. I sure wish I had his patience.

My friend Jon, a teenage boy in our neighborhood, comes to my party a little late. I am so happy to see him. The most exciting thing about my party, for Ma at least, is when Jon paints a portrait of me on the garage wall. Here we are in the middle of a party, dogs running around, music play-ing, and people chit-chatting, when Jon walks right up to the back wall and paints a picture of me. I'm not kidding. And it looks just like me. Everyone claps for him.

Ma has a table set up with what she calls adult bever-ages. My dog friends and me just get water, but that's okay. There's lots of people treats like hotdogs with bacon wrapped around them, and fruit and cheese, and all kinds of crackers and dips. Me and my dog friends celebrate with dog biscuits and little bits of hotdog without the bacon.

Pa lights the candle that's on the top of the cake and everyone sings "Happy Birthday to Bogey." Ma and Pa blow out the candle and everybody laughs and dances around. This is some kind of party.

The party is over. Ma and Pa and me go back into the

house, and I get to play with all my new toys. This is a special day that I will never forget. Too bad birthdays only come once a year.

6

WHAT'S IN a Name?

Boy oh boy, I think Ma and Pa are gonna change my name. I sure hope not cuz I like my name just the way it is. I'm sitting here, listening to their conversation. At the same time I'm praying and praying that they let me keep my name. I don't know why but it seems that Pa is questioning why my other owners named me Bogey.

"Maureen," Pa says. "What do you think they had in mind when they gave Bogey his name? Do you suppose they were Humphrey Bogart fans or do you think they were golfers like us?"

Ma looks at Pa with a quizzical expression on her face. "Who knows? But if it has to do with golf, I'd rather it be Birdie or Eagle. Or how about Albatross? Three under par – God, I'd love to have one of those. But who wants to get a

Maureen O'Brien

bogey on a hole? Not me."

"Birdie and Eagle would be fine for a girl dog," Pa says. "We could come up with a new name, but that wouldn't be fair to him. He's used to Bogey."

Ma and Pa finally decide that my name definitely has to do with golf. And now as I listen more, I realize why Pa was thinking that maybe I should have a name change.

You see, their golfing buddies always comment on my name – mostly negative stuff.

"What kind of a name is that for him? He's such a great dog."

"That name is way too negative. Who wants to be over par?"

"What a shame. You should change his name."

Pa is mulling it over. He always mulls things over before he makes any decisions.

"You know what," he says to Ma. "I say Bogey keeps his name but, we change our response to all those negative comments."

The very next day we run into a guy on our walk and he starts in about my name. Pa says, "No, no you don't understand. Bogey isn't over par, he's above par – way above par. He's so special, there's not another dog quite like him. He's more like a quadruple bogey. It's the perfect name for him."

Pa's pretty smart, don't you think?

7   MY BIG FAMILY

Ma and Pa almost always take me with them on their road trips, especially when Ma is playing in a golf tournament. I get to meet all the fun lady golfers in South Carolina. When we arrive at the golf course for the practice round, the first thing I hear is, "Where's Bogey? I can't wait to see him." These ladies always make me feel special.

But there are times when I have to stay home. Remember the kid in that movie, "Home Alone?" I know it's not a true story but I still feel sorry for that kid. I mean he really was alone. Not me. I'm never home alone for more than six hours. How lucky I am to have such a big, loving family. I have three special Aunties and my very own Nana to take care of me. Sometimes they just take me for walks, and other times I go to their house for a sleepover.

Auntie Marge takes me for lots of walks. She always

Maureen O'Brien

has treats in her pocket. The treats aren't just for me, though. She's very generous with all the dogs in the neighborhood. I don't mind at all cuz she always gives me extras. Sometimes we walk over to her house to pick up her freshly baked muffins. Then we deliver the muffins to all her friends in the neighborhood. Her house always smells so yummy. As soon as I walk into her house, I sit up and do my pretty please pose. With all those smells, I figure she has some kind of special snack for me.

Auntie Marge also has a cat that she keeps on a leash. Her cat never walks with us so I don't understand why she sits in her front yard on a leash. Auntie Marge explains it to me this way, "Babes is an indoor cat. But she likes to be outside in the fresh air every once in awhile, just like you. If I let her loose, she might get lost and we don't want that to happen, right, Bogey?" It makes some sense, I guess. I cock my head to tell her I understand. To tell you the truth, I don't get it at all.

After our deliveries are done, we go back home to my house. Auntie Marge never goes back to her house right away. She stays and plays with me for about an hour. Then she sits down at our kitchen counter and writes notes to Ma. "Five pees, two poops. Bogey and I had a very good walk. He is the best boy I've ever known." I don't understand why she's counting all my business stuff. She used to be a nurse so I guess that's what nurses do. I sure love her.

Auntie George is lots of fun. She takes me for walks but we never go straight home to my house. Instead, we go over to her house. She has two dogs named Tina and Pris and I get to play with them for a few hours. They have more toys than I've ever seen before and they're very good about sharing. Much better about that than me. Tina is the love of my life. It's kind of a secret between us. But I think Auntie George knows how I feel about Tina

Auntie George is a big animal lover. Besides Tina and Pris, she has a cat named Hobo, and two birds. The birds stay in a cage and that kind of makes me sad. I mean I think birds should be allowed to fly around wherever they want to go. Her birds squawk a lot and I swear it sounds like they're saying, "Let me out of here."

Hobo is Auntie George's pride and joy. He's known as the Neighborhood Cat. Everybody's crazy about him, in-

cluding me. Hobo is my hero cuz he's so brave.

I'll never forget the day Hobo saved my life. One day

a stray dog, a very big one, attacked me. I was on my leash and Ma was screaming. I did everything I could to get the upper hand but this dog was way too big for me. Hobo appeared out of nowhere, jumped on that dog's back, and dug his claws in. The dog yelped really loud and ran away with his tail tucked between his legs. We never saw that dog again.

Auntie Lillian takes care of me at her house. I can't tell you how many hours I spend snuggling with her in bed. To tell you the truth, she takes me for such long walks that I'm happy to jump into bed with her when we get home. I need the rest. Auntie Lillian is the only person who gets right down on the floor to play with me. I love doing sleepovers at her house.

What I really love when I'm with Auntie Lillian are all the people we meet on our walks. She goes on and on about all the tricks I can do. Some people don't believe her. When that happens, she raises her voice in protest. "I'm not exaggerating. This boy doesn't just roll over and play dead and stuff like that. He can answer any math problem you give him." I try to tell her that it's all right so I move very close to her side, smile up at her, and wag my tail. Then they ask Auntie to get me to do some tricks. She always says, "He only does them for Moe."

Nana Betty is my one and only Nana. I do more sleepovers with her than anyone else.

I remember when Ma had her back surgery. I lived with Nana for six whole weeks. In the beginning, I really missed Ma. But after a week, I felt so loved that even when we visited Ma, I couldn't wait to go back home with Nana.

Nana likes to grow flowers. She picks them from her gardens outside and puts them in vases in the house so it always smells very pretty. Sometimes I jump up onto a chair and sniff them. That always makes Nana laugh.

When the weather is warm and sunny, Nana and me spend lots of time outside. Daddy Skip, Nana's husband, joins us out there too. They like to sit in their driveway and visit with all the people who walk in the neighborhood.

I always sit right up on Nana's lap. The only problem

Maureen O'Brien

is that most of the walkers have their dogs with them. Of course, Nana being Nana has treats right there on the table for all the dogs. Every time a dog stops by, I jump off her lap and do my pretty please pose. I figure it's my turn to get another treat

"No, Bogey," she says. "You already had yours."

So I jump right back up on her lap and stare down the other dogs. I just wanna make sure that all those dogs know that she is *my* Nana. I guess I'm a little possessive cuz I love her so much.

Nana always calls me her "Special Puppy Pal." Is that cute or what? Next to Ma and Pa, I love my Nana the most of everybody.

Inside every Newfoundland, boxer, elkhound and Great Dane is a puppy longing to climb onto your lap.

— *Helen Thomson*

Maureen O'Brien

I Have a Secret

8

Pa and me are snuggling in his recliner. It's our special time together right before dinner. He's sipping on his cocktail and Ma's in the kitchen, cooking up a storm. Wait a minute, that's an exaggeration. Ma doesn't cook fancy dinners. She only cooks easy, simple meals.

I decide I can't keep it to myself anymore, and so I tell Pa my secret. I put my paws right up on his chest and kiss his ear as I whisper to him. I make him promise not to tell anyone. I don't know if he really understands, but he hugs me so I guess he's happy for me.

Why am I so embarrassed about this? I don't know. I mean, here I am three years old, what's so earth shattering about me having a girl friend? For the first time in my life, I am in love. Yup, you heard it right.

The object of my affection is Tina. She's an Italian

Greyhound who moved into my neighborhood about five months ago. She lives right down the street from me at Auntie George's house. Whenever it's time for me to go for a walk, I hope and pray that she'll be out there with Auntie.

I can't take my eyes off her. Her body is so sleek and her fur so smooth, it looks and feels like silk. Complete opposite of my kinky, curly hair. And then she has these doe-like eyes that beg me to whisper sweet nothings in her ear.

Here's what seals the deal for me. This girl can run fast. I mean really fast, almost as fast as me. Sometimes I let her win a race just so she'll keep playing with me. What a guy, right?

I know what you're thinking right now. I'm a gonner, right? You're right. She's the real deal. This is not puppy love.

Maureen O'Brien

Guess Who Came For Dinner And Stayed?

9

I'm so lucky to be an only child. Maybe I'm even a little spoiled, on account of I don't have to share anything. Ma tells everyone that I'm spoiled rotten. She doesn't usually exaggerate stuff, so I guess she's right.

All the toys around the house are mine. All the treats, too, even the bones. I don't know why I always hide my bones but I do. Maybe in the back of my mind I think someone's gonna sneak in the house and steal them. You're probably thinking I have an over-active imagination. Not true. This really could happen.

Right now, I'm a little more worried than usual. Crazy things are going on in my neighborhood. I might have to go change my hiding places.

Every day for three weeks I watch people up and down my block put food out for a cat that's hanging out in our neighborhood. They probably want her to be their pet. It looks like she's getting more food than me. I'm starting to get a little jealous.

Now that cat is in my house. Well, not exactly in my house, yet, but way too close for comfort. You heard it right. This is not some Cat in the Hat, make believe story. This is a for real story. I told you it could happen.

Probably I shouldn't call it a cat. It's just a tiny version of one. Just as bad if you ask me. I mean a cat is a cat, right?

She's a little ball of dark grey fur, almost black but not quite. Pretty close to my color actually. Her eyes, what little I can see of them, are a kind of a yellow mustard color. And what a racket she makes. Meow, meow, meow is all I hear. When I tell you she's a loudmouth, I'm not exaggerating. I'm like Ma that way, I don't exaggerate.

How did this happen? Well the whole time I'm watching the neighbors feed this cat, I hear Pa tell Ma over and over again, "Don't you put any food or milk out there for that stray." He doesn't want to adopt a cat, that's for sure. I can tell Ma's tempted to feed her, but she has promised Pa that she won't. I know Ma will keep her promise cuz she even told Pa that we can't have a cat on account of she's allergic to them and so am I.

But this cat is very strange. Even though all the neighbors are feeding her, she doesn't stay at their houses or in their yards. Nope, in between meals, she comes to our yard and lulls the day away. It's as if she's decided to eat in one place, but live with us.

I guess Ma can't stand it anymore, cuz today I hear her

Maureen O'Brien

tell Pa that they have to talk about the cat situation. "Honey," she says, "I've been doing some research on cats. It appears that they're quite discerning little critters. They don't just go live with people who are feeding them. Oh no. They adopt the people they want to live with. I think we've been adopted."

Pa leans back in his recliner and laughs so hard I think he's gonna tip the recliner over. "Sweetheart, you're so funny. I guess you're telling me that we might become cat owners. But there's a big problem here. How are you going to handle this with your allergies? And let's not forget about Bogey, he'll be sneezing all day long. I don't think this will work."

"Well," Ma says, "Meow could be an outdoor cat. We could put a...."

Pa raises both arms and puts his hands out in front of him. "Whoa, slow down a minute. Did you just call her Meow? You've already given her a name? Sounds like you've made up your mind."

"I guess I have," Ma says, "I mean it would be such fun, and Bogey would have a little sister to play with. Besides, who wouldn't want to be adopted by a cat? It'll be loads of fun. Like I was about to say, we can put in a pet door to the garage and another one to the enclosed courtyard. This way Meow will have two rooms of her own where she can eat, drink and be merry, and stay out of the elements. And we won't have cat hair all over the house. It'll work out just fine."

After a little more discussion, Ma and Pa agree to be adopted. Then Ma goes out and coaxes Meow to come to her for some cuddling. She picks her up, carries her into the house, and introduces her to me. "Bogey, say hello to your new little sister, Meow. You two are going to become such good friends."

Meow shoves her nose right up to mine and sniffs me all over. It's like she's trying to decide if she wants to be my sister. Some attitude, right? Cats are different, that's for sure.

Ma goes to the store right away and buys some dry cat food and two bowls, one for food and the other for water. I guess this is a done deal.

Mostly Meow eats here now but it looks like some neighbors are still putting food out for her. They haven't given up on her. I think they still want Meow to adopt them.

Today, Ma took Meow to Ark Animal Hospital to have an operation so she won't be able to have babies. Good thinking, there. I hope she doesn't have to wear a crazy cone like I had to.

While she was there, the doctor happens to tell Ma that Meow is a Russian Blue cat. So now, Ma calls her Meowshevik.

For what it's worth, I'm okay with these living arrangements, as long as Meowshevik stays outdoors. Otherwise, I'll have to hide my bones all over again.

10 I'm Not Black Anymore

Ma is here to pick me up at the Diva Dogs Spa. She strokes my back where Uncle Vinnie trimmed me and tilts her head the way I do sometimes when I'm trying to figure something out.

"What's with Bogey's hair?" she says. "Where did all that grey come from? He's not even a year old yet so why is he getting so grey?"

I can't see myself so I don't know what she's talking about. Ma doesn't seem upset or anything, just a little confused.

"That's not grey, Moe," Uncle Vinnie says. "Bogey's hair color is changing to silver. It happens lots of times with black poodles. He's just a handsome silver dude now."

When we get home I just happen to catch a glimpse of me in the hall mirror. Wow, I sure do look different. My hair

Maureen O'Brien

sparkles and glitters now, kind of like the tinsel on a Christmas tree. I agree with Uncle Vinnie. I do look handsome. When Pa and me take our walk, I don't walk, I do my proud prancing moves.

Everyone we see on our walk comments on my new color. One lady says, "He's such a pretty boy."

Not sure I like being called pretty. I don't know about you but I think pretty is for girls and handsome is for boys.

I don't sweat the small stuff though so I just keep prancing.

11

I Did It!

Today is a big day for me. Ma and Auntie George and me are taking a long road trip just so I can take a very important test. I'm so glad Auntie is here cuz I get to sit on her lap in the front instead of in my doggy car seat in the back. Plus, she's giving me all kinds of pet pets which are having a good calming effect. Just what I need right now.

Auntie George and Ma start talking about the Therapy Dog test. "Bogey will do just fine. He knows his stuff," Auntie says.

Ma looks over at me and blows me a kiss. "Oh, I know he does. I just hope there aren't lots of other dogs there. He becomes a little fidgety and loses his focus in situations like that."

I wish I was feeling as confident as Auntie and Ma. I

Maureen O'Brien

mean this is a really hard test. You have to do everything just right. They don't give you any second chances. I mean, if you get one thing wrong, you get a big "F" and then you can't be a Therapy Dog.

Geez, I hope I ace the test. I know how much Ma and Pa want me to be a therapy dog. I just want them to be proud of me.

Right now, I'm trying to remember all the things I have to do right. Instead of that, my brain is churning about all the stuff I did wrong during my training classes. I can't seem to get this stuff out of my head.

I mean here I was just six weeks ago in my second training class. I already knew how to do all the little stuff like, "Sit," "Down," and "Stay." That was easy for me.

But some of the other stuff was really hard. Like meeting another dog and not growling. There was this one dog in the class named Rusty. He's what I call a mixed breed type. Notice I didn't say mutt cuz I think that doesn't sound very nice. I mean, so what if he doesn't have papers. Right?

From the first moment I met Rusty, I didn't like him. He trotted over to me and sniffed my butt. A little sniffing I could deal with, but this guy wouldn't stop. So I let out a pretty big growl. Anything to get him to stop.

The Training Lady ran over to Ma and me and pointed her finger at me. "Be nice, Bogey. No growl," she said. Ma came to my defense right away and explained what had happened, but that didn't seem to matter. Under no circumstances was I to growl at another dog. Let me tell you how I felt about that…. Oh, I can't even go there.

About ten minutes later, Rusty, The Mutt, charged at me again.

"Bogey, sit," Ma said. Of course I did. Like I said, that stuff was easy. Without my butt in the air, Rusty retreated. Thank God, cuz I'm telling you what, I was warming up my growlin' chords. And, yeah, I know what you're thinking. Yes, I did change my mind about Rusty. He was a mutt.

Another really hard thing for me was the "Leave It" command. It didn't matter what I saw on the ground around me, even if it was little hot dog pieces, I had to leave it alone. Now we're talkin' self-discipline. I mean I like hot dogs even better than steak.

The hardest thing for me to learn was to stay with strangers when Ma walked away and disappeared. I was sure she was just around the corner and would be right back, but I got scared every time she did that. So I barked and whimpered until she came back. I didn't think I'd ever get this one right.

Oh boy, we're pulling into a parking lot. "We're here," Ma says. "Okay Bogey, let the games begin."

We enter the test site. I feel calm and confident. No more negative thoughts in my head, just positive thoughts. There are ten other dogs here waiting to take the test. I look around and to my delight, Rusty is not one of them.

The testing people call my name first and I prance and dance my way right through every test situation. That's right, Bogey, "the untrainable, stupid dog," passes the test with flying colors. At the end of the test, Ma and me high five each

Maureen O'Brien

other. One of the testers turns to Ma and says, "You've got a winner here. Your Bogey is something special. He's going to be a great therapy dog."

Now I have a new tag on my collar. It's a yellow circle with big black letters that say "I Am A Therapy Dog."

Dogs teach us many things about being a better person...
that people don't teach.

— Author Unknown

Maureen O'Brien

I'm not Much of a Therapy Dog

12

Uh, oh, I'm afraid I'm a bad therapy dog. Maybe bad isn't the right word? I'm just not good at it. I mean, I passed the test, and I'm certified and registered and all that stuff, but I don't really like doing therapy. Ma has taken me to three different nursing homes now, and I was a little naughty at each one.

I didn't growl at anyone or anything like that. I didn't even touch the food that was left on the floor. And even when this one lady threw her cane at me, I ignored her and kept on walking with Ma. I was really good about that stuff.

The problem came when Ma asked me to sit on a man's lap so he could give me pet pets. When she picked me up to put me on his lap, I squirmed just enough to get loose and jumped right out of her arms. I have to tell you that my landing was perfect. Even the French judge would have given me a high score. I was graceful. Then I did make a little growly sound. Not a real growl at all. Just enough to let Ma know that I didn't want any part of this.

I don't know what's wrong with me. I love sitting on Ma's lap, and I practically live on Pa's lap, but don't ask me to sit on a stranger's lap. I just can't help it. I don't want to do it.

Maybe there's some other way to do therapy. I sure hope so.

Maureen O'Brien

My Second Christmas   13

Something big is about to happen. Oh, yeah, I can smell it. Ma is in a little room she calls her office. The door is closed tight and she won't let me in. That's just not like her. She likes me to stay real close to her. She even taught me a game called "Follow Me." That's where I walk one step behind her, while she sings "Me and My Shadow." I'm pretty darn good at this game, but she sure doesn't want to play it right now.

I have a fair amount of patience, but I have to admit I'm losing it. So I scratch on the door a few times. That doesn't work. Then I lie down real, real close to the door and whimper a little. She still won't let me in. Forever goes by. Finally, the door opens. Out she comes, carrying a bunch of presents.

I follow her into the den and watch as she puts the presents under a tree. I'm not allowed anywhere near this tree.

Every time I go near it, Ma says, "Eh Eh." I think she's afraid I'm gonna lift my leg on it. Believe me, I'm tempted. I mean what's a tree for, right?

Now Ma calls me into the living room. We curl up in the recliner together.

"Bogey," she says, "guess what? Santa's coming tomorrow and he's going to bring you something very special."

As soon as I hear the word special, I know this is a serious conversation. So I cock my head from side to side. You know the move. Ma loves when I do that. She knows I'm listening real hard and trying to understand every word.

Now Ma and Pa are off to bed so I sneak over to the tree. I sniff out every one of Ma's presents. All I can smell is scotch tape. I'm here to tell you that my Ma is a terrible gift wrapper. She uses one whole roll of scotch tape on every present. Hard to believe, right?

Pa's presents always look so nice cuz he pays them at the store to do the wrapping. I sniff one of his pretty boxes and I'm almost positive it's a bone. I can't believe I have to wait until tomorrow.

Then I notice some little gift bags off to one side. I'm praying that my presents from Ma are in those bags. Cuz seriously, I don't wanna have to chew through that tape. I had to do that last year. But, if it comes to that – hey, you gotta do what you gotta do.

I'll tell you something, though. I have no intention of going to bed. I'm staying right out here, close to this tree until Santa comes. Last year I didn't get to see him and I

don't wanna miss him again. Ma and Pa will have to sleep by themselves tonight.

Uh oh, I guess that's not gonna work. Ma's calling me right now. "Bogey, come on good boy. Time for nitey-nite."

Oh well, it was a good idea for a minute.

14

It's a little embarrassing when complete strangers stop Ma and Pa and compliment them on how great it is that I'm a therapy dog. The yellow tag on my collar with big black letters, "I Am A Therapy Dog" kind of gives it away. To skirt the issue that I don't actually do therapy, Ma goes on and on about how proud she and Pa are that I passed the test.

"It's a very difficult test," she says. "Lots of dogs aren't able to learn all the skills. This little baby of ours is very smart."

Then the questions begin. "Does he go to nursing homes?" "Where does he go to do his therapy?" "Have you ever taken him to that nursing home down on Route 707? They would love him there."

"We're still working on that," Ma says. "We haven't decided on the best places to take him yet." I think Ma is a little embarrassed, too.

The major problem, if you remember, is that I don't real-

ly like doing this therapy stuff. I mean I'm sure all the people in the nursing homes are very nice. But I don't know them well at all. When I think about sitting on their laps or lying down in their beds with them, I get very fidgety. I also start to sneeze. Seems like when I'm nervous or don't know what to do, I sneeze. If I could just sit on the floor next to their bed or by their wheelchair and let them pet me, I guess that would be okay.

When I know people really good like Nana Betty and all my Aunties in the neighborhood – that's different. I love sitting on their laps, cuddling with them and smothering them with kisses. They aren't strangers at all, they're family to me.

Something I love to do is learn new tricks. I'm all ears whenever Ma says, "Hey, Bogey, how would you like to learn a new trick?" I'm not really sure what a trick is, but learning new stuff is just plain fun for me. It doesn't hurt that Ma gives me lots of treats when I'm learning. Each time I get it right or even almost right, she gives me little pieces of hot dogs or cheese. Talk about incentives. Then when Ma claps and cheers for me, I just wanna do the trick over and over again. "Bravo, Bogey," she says. "You're so incredible. You are the best boy in the whole universe."

I'm three years old and I know ten tricks. I mean I have them down pat. So Ma comes up with a really super idea. "Bogey, how about we go do some tricks for children and maybe teach them important things at the same time?" I jump up into her arms and kiss her right on the lips. That's how I let her know that I'm happy about something.

That very day Ma calls the Socastee Library in Myrtle Beach and books my first gig at The Children's Story Hour. Don't you love that word "gig?"

This is the beginning of my career as a therapy dog. Like

Ma says, "There are all kinds of ways to do therapy. Making people laugh, and clap, and jump for joy is wonderful therapy for anyone."

Word spreads so fast I can't believe it. Two other libraries call Ma and then three nursing homes and all of a sudden I am doing three gigs every month. One of my favorite gigs is at a high school for a special needs class. Those kids are such fun.

Finally, I have a job to do and I love it.

I think dogs are the most amazing creatures; they give unconditional love.
For me they are the role model for being alive.

— *Gilda Radner*

Maureen O'Brien

CONFESSIONS OF a CATHOLIC DOG

15

Sometimes I do things that Ma thinks are naughty. But Pa doesn't see it that way at all. He just laughs and says, "That isn't naughty, that's funny." It's kind of hard to tell naughty from funny cuz Ma and Pa react to things so differently.

For instance, I am an uncontrollable sock thief. I can't seem to help it. It's an obsession with me. Doesn't matter whether the socks are dirty and smelly or fluffy and clean straight out of the dryer. I probably steal and hide two socks a week. Sometimes even three, if Ma does a lot of laundry.

Because I know Pa thinks it's funny, I let him see me sneaking around with the sock in my mouth. When he's in the living room in his recliner, I sit right in the entrance to the room and wait until he looks up at me. "You little sock thief, you," he says. Then he laughs so hard he has to blow his nose. On the way to my hiding place, I look back to make sure he isn't following me. How I love to hear him laugh.

When Ma's in the house, I do it on the sly. If she catches me in the act, she hollers at me. "Bogey, you are a naughty boy. Bring that sock back to me. Right now." She's such a spoilsport when it comes to socks. I don't like to make her mad so most times I wait until I see her drive off in her car. Then off I go in search of socks.

One of my favorite hiding places for socks is under the pillow in the guest bedroom. Today Ma and Pa have a friend visiting them and she's staying overnight. Wouldn't you know, I forgot to move my socks to another hiding place. Geez, I hope Freda Mae, the lady who is visiting, doesn't notice them. At least, I hope she doesn't tell Ma about them.

Oops, too late. Here comes Freda Mae. She walks into the living room holding up three socks, all different colors. "Moe, look what I found under my pillow. Is this a new way to freshen up a bed? They smell lovely and so does the bed."

I am so embarrassed. Besides which, I just know Ma is going to holler at me.

"I've been looking for those socks for a week," says Ma. Then Ma turns and looks at me. She laughs that wonderful, throaty laugh of hers that I like so much. I don't understand this. Why isn't she mad at me? No wonder I'm so confused between naughty and funny.

Here's another kind of bad thing I do. I help myself to any food left up on the island counter in the kitchen. And I know it's naughty. But it smells so good and it's so easy to

Maureen O'Brien

do. I just jump onto the stool when nobody is looking and Bingo.

There is a McDonald's Big Breakfast on the counter right now. Pa is nowhere to be seen. I devour the pancakes, eggs, and bacon but I leave the biscuit for him. Pretty nice of me, I think. Pa comes back into the kitchen and this time he's not laughing. Now he's yelling at me. I know I am a very bad boy – this is way worse than naughty. My stomach rebels for the rest of the day.

The only other naughty thing I ever do is turn over open waste paper baskets and strew the stuff throughout the house. That is just so much fun. But Ma is a spoilsport on that too. She gets baskets with covers on them so I can't do it anymore.

The more I think about the bad stuff I do, the more I think I'm really not all that bad. Just a little bad.

16

A CLOSE CALL

Ma and me are on our way to see Uncle Vinnie for my haircut. We're taking Pa's car on account of Ma's car is in the repair shop. She just put me in the back seat. Does she really think I'm gonna stay back here?

This is not her car with a doggy car seat for me to sit in. This is Pa's car. And, when I'm in his car, I always sit in the front on Pa's lap, with my head out the window.

About five minutes into the trip, I decide enough is enough. Hey, all I want is to be up front where I belong. I bark and bark, trying to get Ma to understand. Ma pays no attention to me.

We're stopped at a traffic light now. Time for me to make my move. I jump up to get into the front passenger seat, but I'm hung up on the silly headrest. My front side is

Maureen O'Brien

draped over the headrest but my backside is lagging behind. I manage to squirm just enough to get all of me onto the front seat.

Ma yells at me and reaches over with her arm to protect me. Perfect. Just enough room for me to slip under her arm and onto her lap. How do you spell relief? Finally, I'm where I'm supposed to be. Mission accomplished. Not for long, though.

Ma starts to scream like crazy and pulls the car over into a parking lot. She opens the door, drags me out of the front seat and puts me right back into the back seat. She isn't exactly gentle about it either.

"Bogey," she yells even louder. "You stay in the back. And don't you dare move a muscle." She's really mad at me. I don't understand why. I mean, when I'm in Pa's car, I sit up front on his lap. And I am in Pa's car.

She pulls back onto the road and I do what any smart dog would do. Yup, I make the same moves. This time I don't get hung up and here I am, back on her lap.

Ma gives up this time. "Okay, just this one time, Bogey. But you sit still and be good. We're almost there."

I try hard to stay still and be quiet. I really do cuz I know I'm in trouble with Ma. But then I get thinking about how Pa lets me stick my head out the window. I remember how good it feels when the wind blows my ears back and what fun it is to talk to people when we stop at a light.

Ma has the window open a little bit, and I can't stand it anymore. I want my head out that window. So I turn a little sideways and shift my paws onto the armrest. I get my head out the window but just barely. Oh my gosh – the window's moving up really fast, closing in on my neck and squeezing my throat. I'm choking and I can't breathe. It hurts so much. I can't even cry.

Ma acts really fast. I don't know how she does it, but she makes the window go back down and pulls the car off to the side of the road. There's lots of traffic all around us, and people are honking their horns and yelling bad words at her. I'm still gasping for air and coughing.

Ma is crying and shaking. She massages my neck and throat. "Are you okay? It's going to be all right baby," she repeats over and over again. I start to breathe a little better.

Ma is still rubbing my sore neck, but reaches for her phone with her other hand and calls Pa. I'm not paying close attention to what she's saying cuz I'm still hurting, but I know she's asking Pa to come right away to help us. She sounds like she's panting. "I don't know how it happened, Lamar. Somehow, he pressed the window button with his paw. His neck could be broken. Hurry, please!"

We wait for about twenty minutes. I start to feel better but Ma is still sobbing.

"I'm so sorry, Bogey," she says. "It's all my fault. I never should have let you stay on my lap. Dearest Jesus, please let my baby be okay."

Pa is here now. I sit on Ma's lap while Pa drives us to Ark Animal Hospital. At the hospital, Dr. J takes a long time to examine me. She looks very serious as she listens to my breathing. "You are one lucky little boy, Bogey. Do you know that?" I give her a kiss just like I always do.

Ma runs her hands through her hair. "Doctor J, are you sure he's all right? I mean what about broken trachea bones? Should we do an X-ray or anything like that?"

It takes a while but Doctor J finally assures Ma that I am just fine. "It's you I'm worried about, Moe. I think you could use a sedative of some kind. Do you have something at home you could take to calm you down?"

Ma taps her hand on the examining table. "Thanks, I do." She turns and looks at Pa. "Right now I just want to get home – safely."

Ma sits in the back seat with me as Pa drives us home. She's talking non-stop to Pa as she strokes my back. "Don't you ever let Bogey sit in your lap when he's in your car. To-morrow, I'm going to buy another doggy car seat just for your car. He is precious cargo and we can't take chances ever again."

I think Doctor J is right. I am lucky to be alive.

17 THE WORST FIVE WEEKS OF MY LIFE

February 11, 2010

M a is crying and it looks like she can't stop. I try
everything I know to make her feel better, but
so far, nothing is working. Usually when she's
sad about something, all I have to do is sit on her lap and give
her lots of kisses. Then she hugs me and puts on her happy
face and tells me how much she loves me. Not today.

Now she's yelling at somebody. I don't know who cuz
it's just the two of us in the house. "Oh God, Oh God," she
screams over and over again. I can't figure this out cuz she's
usually so soft spoken.

To see her like this is so upsetting to me. So I leave her
and go into the front bedroom. Maybe she just needs to be
alone. Besides, in here I can sit up on the bed, look out the

window, and watch Pa's car in the driveway. I'm praying that he'll get out of his car and get in here. Ma really needs him right now. I do, too.

It seems like an eternity goes by and still no Pa. Ma is still crying in the living room. At least she's not yelling and screaming anymore.

There is a silence in the house now and Ma comes in and sits next to me on the bed. I turn away from the window and look at her, hoping she's not crying anymore. I kiss the tears that are running down her cheeks.

"Bogey, Pa has gone to heaven," she says. "He's gone, baby."

March 20, 2010

It's been about five weeks now and I'm still looking for Pa. I can smell him everywhere. I don't understand why I can't find him. I feel so lonely and so sad. I don't eat the food that Ma puts out for me every day. I feel itchy and restless and can't sleep at all. There is no fur left on my right leg. All I see is skin and bone. I can't seem to stop chewing. I stay on Pa's recliner all day and all night, waiting for him to come back.

Ma takes me for walks but my usual strong legs start to buckle so I can't really go that far.

Ma takes me to see Doctor J today and she says that I'm mourning. She gives Ma some pills for me to take.

"These are anti-depressants," Doctor J says. "They

should help him a little." She also gives Ma some ointment for my leg. She tells Ma that it might be a long time before I get over this.

I don't think I'll ever get over this. I want my Pa back.

Maureen O'Brien

A New Normal?

18

I'm lyin' on my back up on Ma's bed while she checks on my leg. She has that ointment tube in her hand, which is just about empty. She strokes my leg and then rubs my belly. Boy, does that feel good.

"Hey sweet baby, I think your leg is all better," she says. "How about that. All your hair has grown back. You're doing great. No more ointment for you." I roll over, sit right up and kiss her smack dab on her lips. Ma loves when I do that. "You are a French poodle, aren't you? That was quite a kiss, baby boy."

I follow her into the kitchen, as usual, just two steps behind her. She turns and holds the ointment tube up to me, before throwing it in the garbage. "See, all gone. Too bad they don't have an ointment that could make me all better."

Ma washes the breakfast dishes and then motions me to follow her. "Bogey, c'mon. Let's go chill a little." I follow her into the living room and hop up onto her lap in the recliner. She's giving me some serious pet pets now. "Bogey, we have to get back to normal, sweet baby." She repeats this, over and over again. I cock my head cuz I'm really trying to understand her.

Back to normal? What's with that, I'm thinking? Normal is when Pa is here. When he takes me for walks every day. Yeah, normal is when Pa brings leftover scrambled eggs home for me from the diner. And where are Pa's socks that he leaves on the floor right next to his side of the bed so I can steal them? That's normal. Or how about the vanilla ice cream that Pa shares with me every night? All that stuff is normal but it's not happening. I mean, how can I get back to normal when Pa isn't here?

Ma must be reading my mind, or something. I swear she must, cuz all of a sudden, she gives me this big hug and says, "Okay, enough chilling for me. For you, too. Anyway, we haven't really been chilling, we've been moping. Pa wouldn't want us to mope, Bogey. C'mon baby, we need to get out of this funk. Let's start a new normal."

For the rest of the day, Ma looks like she's almost dancing, compared to the way she's been moving around the house. She's humming a lot too. It's like a heavy fog that she couldn't see through, is starting to lift.

So far, today is a pretty good day. You know what? I think tomorrow's gonna be even better.

Maureen O'Brien

A Surprise Car Trip
19

At this very moment, I'm watching Ma really close. She doesn't know it. She thinks I'm sound asleep up here in Pa's recliner but I do have my eye on her. I always have my eye on her. She walks toward me with my harness and leash in her hand.

"Hey, sweet baby, how would you like to go for a ride in Ma's car?"

I'm so excited I can't stand it. I sit up, wag my tail and jump into her arms. Then I jump down and do a big Yoga stretch. Well, that's what Ma calls it anyway…yeah, I stretch out both back legs, one at a time, really far back. I'm ready now for a car ride. I'm always ready for that.

I'm in my doggie car seat and I have no idea where we're going. I think it's gonna be some kind of surprise. Ma's got some happy music playing on the car radio and she's singing along, really loud. Ma's not usually loud except when she's doing a sing-a-long. The other thing is that she never knows the words to the song, so she makes them up. That's okay with me. It's been a while since I heard her sing. And, here she is singing again. I love hearing that crazy, deep, throaty voice of hers.

Here we are at a stop light. Ma takes her hands off the wheel and starts to clap to the music. "Hey Bogey, c'mon sing with Ma," she says. "You're going to love where we're going. It's going to be such fun." I start to sing but Ma's voice is drowning me out. Boy, she sure does sing loud.

Ma's parking the car now and my nose is twitching like crazy. I can't quite make out what I'm smelling, but I think it's salt. Yup, it is salt. Then my ears perk up cuz I hear something that sounds a little familiar. The waves are rolling in, that's what I'm hearing. Oh my gosh, we're at the beach. We haven't been to the beach in such a long time. This is gonna be a happy day.

I love the beach, and I know it sounds crazy, but I don't go in the water. Ma always tells people that I'm kinda different cuz I really don't like the water. After it rains, I don't even like to go out for a walk on account of the puddles. She says that poodles are water dogs. But this poodle is not, and I repeat is not a water dog.

I am so happy here, wrapped in my beach towel, snuggling with Ma and enjoying the sounds and smells of the beach. If this is the new normal Ma was talking about, I'm all for it. I kiss Ma's cheeks to let her know how happy I am.

Maureen O'Brien

Life is gonna be good again.

20

I Am a Show-Off

A s soon as I learn a new trick, I can't wait to do it for anyone and everyone who happens to be around. I don't need a special audience at all. I guess you could call me a show off. And you know what, I think you might be right. Being a show off kind of sounds like a bad thing, but I don't think of it like that. I mean if you can do something really special, shouldn't you show people?

Dancing, singing, jumping through hoops, shaking hands, playing dead, rolling over, saying please, and all that stuff – those are my little tricks. They're good tricks and all, and the kids at the library really like them. But I do have a couple of BIG tricks that Ma calls "gems." When I do these tricks, people clap really loud. They cheer, and shout out stuff like, "Wow," and "Bravo." Sometimes they say, "Oh my good-

Maureen O'Brien

ness." But when they say, "Awesome"I know it's a gem.

I'm not braggin', honest I'm not. I just wanna tell you about some of my favorite gems. Okay, here we go.

My first gem – I read from flashcards. Yep, you heard it right. Ma has four flashcards with a command written on each one. You really gotta picture this. I sit right at Ma's feet and when she shows me a card, I do whatever the card says.

One card says, "Say Please," so I get into my pretty please pose, sitting back on my haunches and raising my legs in the air, with my paws curled under. The next card says, "Give Me High Fives," and I sit back again, but this time I lift both legs up as high as I can and wave them toward her really fast. Then she holds up the "Lie Down" card and, yeah, you guessed it. The last card says, "Jump Up," and so, quick as a bunny, I jump up onto her lap. The audience goes crazy with this one.

Another gem that gets people shaking their heads is when I do arithmetic. Ma asks me to add, subtract, multiply and even divide. Right away, I bark out the answer. These are not just simple arithmetic questions like two plus two either. She asks me hard stuff like four times two and of course, I bark eight times. Twelve divided by two? I get that one right too. I don't know for sure, but I think I might be gifted in arithmetic.

These last two gems are the ones that the library kids like the best cuz they do them right along with me. Or maybe I should say I do them right along with them. Ma asks me and the kids, "What do you do before you cross the street?"

The kids yell out, "Look both ways." While they're saying that, I stand right where I am and look both ways. I turn my head all the way to the right and then all the way to the left. Then I do it a second time. The kids love it cuz they think they're teaching me something. Don't you love it?

This last gem is probably my favorite. At the end of every gig I do, Ma always says how nice everyone was to clap for me the way they did. She always tells the kids that clapping like that shows they have good manners. Then she asks me to show my good manners.

"Bogey," she says, "Can you give the audience some clap-claps?" I roll over on my back and clap my paws together. I do this over and over again so while they're clapping for me, I'm clapping for them. That one is so much fun.

Oh, wait a minute. Let me tell you about this one that the kids really like. Ma brings about six of my toys with us to the gig. Each of my toys has a name and I know all the names. So while I sit and stay, she moves away from me and shows the kids each toy and tells them what they're called. Then she puts all the toys on the floor and she asks the kids which toy they want me to get and bring back. If they say Kermit, I go get Kermit. When they say Star Bright, I bring Star Bright back. We go through all the toys, even Pluto and Puppy Pal, and I don't miss a one. I think the kids like this one the best cuz they're playing the game right along with me.

I love showing off and doing all my tricks, especially for the kids. But the best part is at the very end when Ma tells the kids that, if they want to, they can come up, one at a time and give me pet pets.

At my last gig at The Surfside Library, this little boy is the last one to come up. He walks up to me very slowly and looks a little scared. He pets me on the top of my head so gently. So I look right up at him and give him a big smile.

"He doesn't smile for everyone," Ma says. "Bogey thinks you're a very special boy. He loves you."

The little boy looks at me and says, "I love you, Bogey."

That's even better than clap-claps.

21 How I Learned Japanese

All our neighbors are braggin' on me big time now. They're always talking about all the tricks I do so they know I'm pretty darn smart. But, believe it or not, now they think I speak Japanese.

Ma and me go out this morning for our daily constitutional around the neighborhood. We stop and chat with everyone just like we always do. Of course, everyone is happy to see me and they give me all kinds of pet pets which make me feel really special. I'm sure it makes them feel happy too.

We turn the corner and who do I see but my Auntie Marge walking out of her house. She always has treats in her pocket for me. She gives them to other dogs in the neighborhood, too, but she always gives me extras. I'm pretty sure I'm her favorite. Oops, I'm digressing here.

Back to Auntie Marge. As soon as I see her, I can't hold

back my excitement, so I pull real hard on my leash. Ma can't hold on to it, so she lets the leash go. I am free and I know it.

As I run toward Auntie, out of the corner of my eye, I catch a glimpse of a rabbit. I totally abort my original mission and give chase. Let me tell you something, rabbits are a lot faster than they look.

"Bogey," Ma screams. "Come. Here."

I'm on a hunt so I pay no attention to her. I keep my eyes on the bunny. All I can see right now is his little, white bobtail. I know I'm losing ground.

Ma screams even louder, "Bogey, get over here right now. Come."

I continue my pursuit. I never even look back at her.

At this point, Ma panics or something cuz she hollers something in a language I've never heard before. It sounds like gobbledygook gibberish, with some kind of up and down lilt to it. It's so different that it gets my attention. I run as fast as I can right back to her.

By this time, five other neighbors dash out of their homes. I think they're afraid that something bad has happened to Ma. To tell you the truth, I'm thinking the same thing.

"Moe," one of the neighbors says, "What did you just say to Bogey? I mean he came running back to you so fast."

Without missing a beat, Ma says, "Oh that – that's Japanese for come."

"Oh my God," the neighbor says. "I know Bogey's smart but this is incredible. He understands Japanese. I've seen everything now."

Maureen O'Brien

I See A Colorful Bridge

22

I don't feel too good this morning. I'm very weak, and I have no energy. How could this be?

It was just yesterday that I did a gig at the Grand Strand Nursing Home. I felt great then. I did a bunch of tricks for everyone and they laughed, and cheered, and clapped like crazy. I even had them singing, "Do, Re, Mi," with me. And then I went around to everyone and sat right by their wheelchairs so they could pet me. It was such fun. I'm so glad I've become a good therapy dog.

So how could I feel this bad the very next day? No pain or anything like that but I just want to sleep all the time. I walk over to my food and sniff at it but it doesn't smell good to me. I don't feel like eating at all. I try to drink some water. I dip my tongue in the water, but that's about it. I'm having a hard time swallowing.

Ma knows that I'm not myself and she seems worried. I can tell cuz when she asks me if I want to go for a ride in her car, she doesn't have any fun in her voice. Now I know why....Our car ride ends at Ark Animal Hospital.

Doctor J and Doctor Andrews come to see me in the examining room. I'm thinking this must be something serious cuz usually I only get to see one doctor. They take turns examining me, pressing here and there and taking my temperature. They listen to my heart and my lungs. Nothing hurts when they do this so I just keep smiling and licking their hands. I know all about this stuff cuz that's what the doctor does when I go for a check-up every year. They are both so gentle. Then they talk to each other and leave Ma and me alone in the room.

Ma leans over the table and hugs me very gently. "It's going to be all right, sweet baby. You know the doctors will find out what's wrong. I promise you, they'll fix it. Okay, baby. You just rest right now. Everything is going to be just fine."

Doctor J comes back into the room.

"Moe, our Bogey doesn't feel good, that's for sure." She always says our Bogey cuz I'm kind of like the mascot for this hospital. "Let me run a few tests, and keep him here and watch him for the day. I think he's pretty dehydrated so we'll get some fluids into him and give him some antibiotics."

Ma doesn't want to go home without me. "What do you

Maureen O'Brien

think the problem is? Maybe I should stay here with him."

It takes awhile, but Dr. J finally convinces Ma that I'll be just fine and tells her to go home. She promises to call as soon as she has more information.

I spend five hours at the hospital where they have me hooked up to something that gives me fluids and they're taking lots of blood out of me. Well, it seems like a lot. And boy are they ever watching me. I mean, someone comes by my crate about every five minutes and pets me and talks to me. It's very nice and all, but I really don't feel like visiting right now. I'm very, very tired. They take me out to do my business but I'm having a hard time walking.

When Ma comes to get me, Doctor J says I can go home now but that Ma has to watch me very closely. She says something about my kidneys and liver not working too good. She also tells her that she gave me an antibiotic shot. The Doctor gives Ma some pills to give me tomorrow.

Doctor J says, "If he gets any worse, call me right away. We're here until eight o'clock. After that, call the Emergency Hospital and take him there immediately."

That night I try to get up onto the bed to go nitey-nite with Ma but I can't jump up. So Ma lifts me up onto the bed. We snuggle together and it feels good to me even though I still don't feel good. She keeps the bedside table lamp on so she can really watch me. At eleven o'clock, my tummy hurts and I start to whimper and cry really loud. Ma calls the Emergency Hospital immediately, and they tell her to bring me right in. Then she calls Auntie George and asks her to come with us.

We get there and the doctor says that Ma needs to leave me. They will watch me and continue with the antibiotics and give me more fluids. They tell her to go home and call in the morning.

Ma comes back the very next morning. This time Auntie Lillian is with her. I'm feeling even worse. I'm not sure what they say to Ma but I hear her screaming and crying. "How could this be? He was just fine two days ago. He did a gig at the nursing home. Isn't there something you can do for him? What happened to him? Why is this happening?"

The next thing I remember, Ma is holding me on her lap, stroking my body from head to tail, and singing to me. She has this special song she sings to me every day.

"How much is that Bogey in the mirror? The one with the prettiest eyes. How much is that Bogey in the mirror? I do hope he'll be my surprise." She always sings that song to me while we sit at the edge of her bed with the dresser mirror right in front of us. As soon as she says surprise, I give her a kiss. It takes every ounce of energy I have right now but when I hear surprise, I lift my head up and kiss her.

Now I feel a tiny prick in my skin. It doesn't hurt at all. I take a very short nap and when I wake up, I feel good again and full of energy. The scenery I see is beautiful and makes me feel peaceful. There is so much to take in. A bridge with a brilliant rainbow around it and grass, the color of green I have never seen. There are colorful flowers everywhere I look and so many birds, singing the prettiest songs.

Dogs and cats are romping about, playing together and having such fun. They run toward me and invite me to play with them. Then they tell me that I'm at the Rainbow Bridge and that soon enough, we'll all cross over to the other side.

What happens next is amazing. I hear a very familiar voice coming from the other side of the bridge. I look over and who do I see but Pa. Oh my gosh, there he is and he's calling out to me.

"Bogey, oh my God, Bogey. I've missed you so much. Come on sweet baby boy. Come and see your Pa. You're going to love it here in heaven with me."

Animals share with us the privilege of having a soul.

— *Pythagoras*

Maureen O'Brien

In Heaven Now   23

I've been up here in heaven with Pa for three weeks now. Pa looks just like he did when I sat on his lap on the drive home from the Humane Society. Maybe even younger than that. I don't know, it's hard to tell cuz everyone looks kind of young. Everyone's happy and nobody's sick or in pain or walking around with crutches or in wheelchairs or anything like that. But I still miss Ma so much.

You're not gonna believe this but right after I ran across the Rainbow Bridge to hug Pa, who did I see but Tina. She was running toward me like she was in a race or something. You remember Tina, don't you? My one and only girlfriend. I remember when she got sick, and all of a sudden, she wasn't out walking with her Ma in the neighborhood. I missed her so much and I didn't know where she went. Ma and Pa kept telling me that she had gone to heaven but that didn't mean anything to me. Just like I didn't understand it when Ma told me that Pa had gone to heaven. Now that I'm in heaven, I get it. There are lots of other dogs here to play with. Cats, too. But Tina and I have picked up right where we left off. We are inseparable, running circles around all the other dogs here.

Guess who else is here? I couldn't believe my eyes when I saw Auntie Marge walk down this pretty, flower-lined street here in heaven. There were so many dogs following her. Just like always, her pockets were filled with doggie treats. "There's my sweetest baby. Bogey, come over here this minute and give me a big hug. Oh my, I've missed you so much." I ran up to her and jumped into her arms. I couldn't stop kissing her.

Another nice thing about heaven is that everybody gets along so nice. No arguments or squabbles, just nice soft voices all the time. Kind of like when I did my library gigs and I heard the lady at the desk tell people to use their library voice. Yeah, everybody here has a library voice.

I've been watching Ma the whole time I've been up here. She's very sad but is trying to make believe she's doing all right. Pa and I are the only ones who know she's not doing good. I'm trying to figure out a way to make her happy again. Pa told me that time will help, but I really don't think so.

Every day she walks into the house and says, "Hi, Bogey. Ma's home. I love you sweet baby." I know that she knows I'm not there. She's just pretending that I am. I keep trying to tell her that I'm up here with Pa in heaven and that I love her and miss her, but she's not listening. She seems very lost

Maureen O'Brien

right now.

Then what does she do but lower her voice to a whisper on account of she knows I don't like loud voices. Ma and Pa have always had these soft voices, which I really loved. So now she almost whispers her greeting again and I'm trying so hard to tell her how much I love her right back. I know she finally hears me cuz she says, "I love you, too, my best baby in the whole universe."

Ma never said the whole world, it was always the whole universe. Is that the sweetest thing you ever heard? I mean the universe is pretty darn big.

I can't wait for her to come and join me and Pa in heaven. We'll be a family again.

24 MY SISTER MAGGIE

Pa and me watch Ma every single day from up here in heaven. For a while there we were thinking she would never have a happy face again. Well, guess what? She's got a new baby now and she's as happy as she can be. Of course, I'm extra happy cuz now I have a little sister.

My sister's name is Miss Maggie Mae Malone. I gotta believe that's way too big a name for such a little pipsqueak. Thank God, Ma mostly calls her Maggie or sometimes Magpie. And even Maggaroni. I can't believe how darn cute she is. I have to admit that if she wasn't my sister and I was still living down there with Ma, I'd probably ask her to be my girlfriend.

She's a redheaded toy poodle. Sopping wet, she only weighs eight pounds. Compared to me at seventeen pounds,

Maureen O'Brien

she's really teeny.

It took Ma so long to decide to get another baby. All her friends and neighbors kept telling her that she should but she said, "No, there will never be another Bogey. Besides which, I don't think I could ever love another dog the way I loved Bogey."

First Ma went back to the Grand Strand Humane Society, the same place where she adopted me. She was being a little picky cuz she was looking for a small puppy who didn't shed, on account of she's allergic. Mostly there were big dogs and the little ones that were there didn't have poodle hair like mine. Hyperlergic hair or something like that. She went back three times and then went to a place called St. Francis in Georgetown a few times. She even got on the computer looking for just the right puppy to adopt. She really wanted to adopt a baby and not just buy one from the store.

A few weeks went by and Ma had just about given up. Then the phone rang and it was Uncle Vinnie from the Diva Dogs Spa. That's where I used to go to get my hair cut. Ma had told Uncle Vinnie that she was ready to adopt and that if he came across a dog that needed a good home….

"Moe," Uncle Vinnie said. "How would you like a one year old red toy poodle? She comes from a long line of show dogs and my mother-in-law, Annie, would like you to have her. She'd practically give her away, but only to you."

So Ma said, "Why would she do that? She's a poodle breeder, isn't she? I'm sure she could get a lot of money for her. Besides I'm really not interested in a show dog."

"Annie met you and Bogey at Ark Animal Hospital," Uncle Vinnie said. "It was just a few days before you had to put Bogey to sleep. You probably don't remember her. But she thought you were so sweet with Bogey and that he was one of the most handsome poodles she'd ever seen. When I told her you had lost him, she asked me to give you a call."

The very next day Ma went over to Annie's house. She couldn't believe her eyes when she pulled into the driveway. About twenty poodles of every size, shape, and color ran up to greet her.

Maggie wasn't outside with the pack. She was in the house sitting like a prima donna on the armrest of a recliner. Ma went into the house with Annie and entered the living room. As soon as she sat on the couch across from Maggie, what did Maggie do but hop off the chair and jump onto Ma's lap. That was that. It took all of ten minutes for Ma to fall in love once again.

The very first thing Ma did was get Maggie a regular "teddy bear" poodle haircut. All the show hair came off. Then Ma changed her name from Kissey to Maggie Mae. Her papers said Kissey and the name actually suited her cuz all she wanted to do was slather everyone with kisses. She still does that even though Ma changed her name to Maggie. I guess she doesn't understand the name change.

Of course everyone in the neighborhood tried to compare Maggie to me. "Do you think she's as smart as Bogey?" "Will she become a therapy dog?" "Will you be teaching her lots of tricks?"

Ma kept repeating, "There'll never be another Bogey. This is Maggie and she's very different. She's just as smart as Bogey I'm sure but …She's not a replacement."

Well, here's my take on Maggie. She's as smart as a whip but she's pretty stubborn. It's not that she doesn't wanna please Ma and make her happy. She really does but she wants to do it her very own way. She's all girl as far as I can tell. She's also very hyper and needs to be the center of attention. The girl never stops, especially if there's a ball around. She'll do anything and everything to get you to play catch with her.

Ma kept telling everyone that Maggie has ADD or OCD or something like that cuz she has to be on the go and playing all the time. I think she has IWP which means "I Wanna Play." She sure keeps Ma busy and most of all she makes her so happy. Ma describes her this way, "Maggie is a personality kid and the most joyful dog I have ever parented."

You know what they say, "If Mama's happy, everybody's happy." Something like that anyway. Well, I'm here to tell you that Pa and me couldn't be happier.

Maureen O'Brien

No matter how little money and how few possessions you own, having a dog makes you rich.

— *Louis Sabin*

25 I Visited Ma Last Night

Today is April 18. That's the day Ma and Pa got married, fifteen years ago. That was a long time ago – I wasn't even born yet. Anyway, me and Pa were cuddling together up here in heaven and we started talking about Ma. We still missed her a lot but we were both so glad she had her happy face on again.

Since it was their anniversary day, Pa was telling me all about their wedding day. "Nothing formal," he said. "Actually very informal. We got married on the practice green at the golf course. Remember how your Ma and I loved teddy bears? That was one of the reasons we adopted you. You looked just like a teddy bear that day we met you at the Humane Society." He giggled. "By the way you still do, little guy."

I rolled over on my back so Pa could give me some belly rubs while he continued his story. "Well, we had a few of our

Maureen O'Brien

very favorite teddies sitting in a little red wagon, right there next to the minister. I know it sounds a little crazy, but those teddies were the symbolic witnesses to our marriage. Then a few years later, who do we meet up with, but you. And you know what, sweet baby boy? You changed our lives forever."

The more Pa told me about the memories of his special day with Ma, the more I missed her. So I started thinking about what I could do to let Ma know how much I loved her.

That's when I made up my mind to visit Ma. Ma has always loved to look at clouds. I guess you could call her a cloud reader. She and Pa would be out walking and she'd look up at the sky. "Lamar, look at that cloud up there. Do you see that bird, sitting on a perch? Isn't that beautiful?" I always got a kick out of the way Ma could see things in clouds.

That's when I knew I had a good idea. I told Pa what I was going to do. He looked at me, stroked my head, and smiled. "Go for it, Bogey. Ma will love that."

So last night when Ma was taking my new sister Maggie for a walk, I tucked myself into one of the white fluffy clouds. The clouds were floating around pretty good. I positioned myself perfectly so Ma could see me. For a while there I thought she would never look up. Then, just as her eyes looked up towards heaven, the cloud I was in broke up and formed into three separate clouds. A magical thing happened. Maybe it was even a miracle. There I was in all three clouds. It was just as clear as it could be. I was face on in one, side profile in another, and running in the third one.

Ma picked Maggie up in her arms and screamed with

delight. "Look, Maggie, there's your brother. Bogey came to visit us."

That was the best present I could have ever given Ma.

Maureen O'Brien

"We give dogs time we can spare, space we can spare and love we can spare. And in return, dogs give us their all. It's the best deal man has ever made.

— M. Facklam

ABOUT
MAUREEN O'BRIEN

Having lived in Myrtle Beach, SC, for the past 28 years, Maureen "Moe" O'Brien considers herself a Southerner. Originally from Mamaroneck, NY, and Bethel, CT, she has settled in to the relaxing, laid-back style of southern living.

Her "claim to fame," as she likes to call it, is having played professional basketball with The Texas Cowgirls and touring with The Harlem Globetrotters in 1959. An avid golfer, she is a two-time SC Senior Golf Champion.

Her book, *Who's Got The Ball? And Other Nagging Questions About Team Life*, published by Jossey-Bass, is a "how to" for team members in all types of work environments. Her poem "A Prayer For Newtown" was recently published in *The Shine Journal*.

A passionate dog lover, she lives with Miss Maggie Malone, her precious redheaded toy poodle. She is a proud grandma to eight granddaughters, all of whom share her love for dogs.

Made in the USA
Charleston, SC
17 October 2015